# JUSTICE UNRAVELED

## My Experience with the Minnesota Legal System – When Ethics Failed

By

Becky A Cole

Edition: First

ISBN: 979-8-89397-815-5

Published by Booklyn Writers

# Acknowledgment

An attorney once told me that the judge can't require an attorney to produce evidence. I get that, but this judge still made his rulings without it, when he should have been throwing out or setting aside the claims that weren't supported with it.

Thank you to the judicial clerk who said I could use information on the judge because it was public information.

Thank you to the staff at OLPR for wanting integrity in your office by asking that the director be removed. Even though your request wasn't honored, it's good to know there are some people who know the difference between right and wrong.

# Foreword

I hired an attorney to help me deal with an unfortunate experience with my landlord, and hiring the attorney turned out to be a mistake. Not because my case didn't have merit, but because it became clear that his sole intention was to just take my money and run – just as he had done with another tenant in the building.

I kept asking where his evidence was that said something different, but it never happened because it wasn't there to be had.

This all started because I asked for my money back.

So, instead of just returning the $3,000 to me, he proceeded to use the court as his playground to end up incurring more than $150,000 in expenses from all sides and got rewarded for it, and he did it with no justification and no evidence.

He insisted I hired him to get me out of the lease of my apartment, but the evidence – including his own – doesn't support that. When I asked the judge why his lack of evidence didn't matter, I got ignored.

He insisted he was "irreparably harmed" because I was somehow able to "force" him to take cash as part of his retainer, but the evidence he provided doesn't support that. It shows him giving me a choice and me accepting a choice he was offering. When I asked the judge how anyone could "force" an attorney to take a retainer and why his lack of evidence didn't matter, I got ignored.

He insisted that it was my fault he was on probation, despite the fact that there were six others he also harmed at the time who were part of his probation, too. When I asked the judge why he was allowed to let this stand, I was ignored.

He filed a motion in court that said he was allowed to file false claims in court because OLPR hadn't told him it was wrong to do so. In theory, filing false claims should have been a probation violation, but it wasn't, and the judge allowed him to continue doing it.

He admits to an ethics violation by telling the court he discussed the case of a previous client with me. It didn't happen. I learned what he did to the other tenant by reading the court records. It is breathtaking to think he is proud of how he handled that case and had he actually told me about it when he said he did, I would have never hired him. Yet, the judge rewarded him for making that claim.

His own attorney said he deserved to be rewarded because I hurt his feelings when I filed the complaint with OLPR, and the judge agreed.

He never denied his conduct. He just didn't want anyone to call it wrong. And he had a village supporting him.

Despite having no supporting evidence, no justification for his conduct, admitting to ethics violations, no documentation in the court records to support his claims, and a settlement arrangement that makes no sense, the judge still saw fit to award him a judgment against me of $18,000.

# About The Author

Becky has a lifetime of being involved in the community. She has received national and local awards and acknowledgments for her volunteer work.

# About the book/Introduction

I moved to Minnesota because of a job offer, and when that work ended, I chose to stay. Never in my wildest dreams did I ever imagine there would be so many challenges in finding housing where I'd be able to stay put. Moving so much wasn't in my plans, but it became necessary because of encounters with unfortunate landlords and conditions with the properties.

However, it was the legal system that was a stunning failure at multiple turns. Housing law for rental housing is pretty clear in Minnesota, so it should have been relatively easy to get some sort of accountability for my experience with my last landlord.

Instead, I found myself in the middle of a great deal of dysfunction, misinformation, and no justification for how I was treated not only by the attorneys but the court and the Office of Lawyers Professional Responsibility. The court turned into a playground and each time I asked the judge why the opposing side wasn't required to have evidence, all I got was ignored.

I ended up with an attempt of being forced into a "settlement arrangement" (I refuse to call it an agreement) that I didn't consent to because I had no knowledge of it, (and there is no evidence I knew of it or consented to it) makes no sense, wasn't in writing, and is not even in the court transcript.

And yet none of that mattered.

# TABLE OF CONTENTS

# Chapter 1

# The Unexpected Journey

## The Minneapolis Move

It was a gray, uneventful morning when my phone rang, breaking the silence in my tiny apartment. I remember Stari half-expecting another call from a telemarketer. To my surprise, the voice on the other end wasn't trying to sell me car insurance—it was offering me a new adventure.

"Would you be interested in moving to Minneapolis to work on a nationwide software rollout as a technical writer?" the voice asked casually as if moving was no more dramatic than switching from one brand of cereal to another. I had never been to Minneapolis before—never even thought of it as more than a cold spot on the map. But something about the offer sparked a curiosity deep inside me. Maybe it was the promise of a fresh start, or maybe I just needed to shake things up.

I quickly had the essentials sorted: an apartment lined up, logistics planned for moving my two cats, and a sense of excitement bubbling beneath my nerves. The apartment I found was a tidy one-bedroom, just three blocks from my new workplace. I hadn't even stepped foot in Minnesota yet, but I had already convinced myself this was going to be the adventure I'd been waiting for.

The apartment building was nothing fancy—brick and simple—but its best feature was its proximity to work. I could practically roll out of bed and land at my desk. For a while, it felt like a good place to settle in.

I remember the first time I set foot in the building's community room, a cozy space with just the right amount of charm. It wasn't luxurious, but it had everything you'd need for hosting gatherings and tables perfect for game nights or dinner parties. Before long, I was using it regularly to host all sorts of gatherings. For the first time in ages, it felt like I was building something—a life that was uniquely mine.

The work itself wasn't too bad either. It had its ups and downs, as all jobs do, but it was steady, and I found a rhythm. Each day, I'd make the short walk to the office. The city, with its chilly winds and its endless stretches of sky, started to feel more like home.

For a while, life in Minneapolis was going smoothly. Sure, the winters were as brutal as the rumors, but nothing a thick coat and a little perseverance couldn't handle. My two cats—Mau Mau and Simon—were settling in, too, lounging in the sunbeams that streamed through the windows during the brief moments when the sun decided to grace us with its presence. I liked to think they were adapting to city life just as I was, finding their own routines in our new home.

But as anyone who's ever uprooted their life knows, the honeymoon phase doesn't last forever. There's always something lurking around the corner, waiting to shake things up. I just didn't expect it to eventually come in the form of so many noisy neighbors, careless landlords, and other nonsense.

For now, Minneapolis felt like a new beginning. The city itself had a quiet charm—nothing flashy, but dependable, like an old sweater you find at the back of your closet and wonder why you hadn't worn it more often. It fit. And that was enough for me for a while.

Everything seemed to be falling into place, and though I had yet to discover the darker side of apartment living, at that moment, I was content. Life, like that perfect cup of coffee, had just the right balance of warmth and bite.

## Apartment Woes Begin

The shine of Minneapolis began to fade around the time I moved into my second apartment. It started off promising—decent location, affordable rent, and, best of all, it was on a bus line, which was critical since I still didn't own a car. I thought I had lucked out, but you know what they say: not all that glitters is gold. In this case, the "gold" was more like a fool's gold wrapped in thin apartment walls.

Then started a string of unfortunate experiences with landlords.

My next apartment was in a decent location and on a bus line, which was important since I didn't have a car yet. However, one of the "features" of this place was that it was a basement apartment, and my window was level with the front porch. No one told me when I signed the lease that it would mean residents of the building would be sitting outside drinking and being loud until all hours of the night.

There was a pause on the other end of the line, followed by a sigh that sounded like it had come from someone who had long ago given up on caring.

"They have a right to drink if they want," he said as if this was the final word on the matter. "As long as they're not breaking the law, there's not much I can do."

After some negotiations, my landlord agreed to let me out of my lease. However, moving meant more money again. Money for a new security deposit and money for movers, but it was necessary as it was clear that the quiet enjoyment I was supposed to be getting wasn't going to happen.

## The Garage and a New Manager

By this time I had become something of an expert in the fine art of apartment hunting. I could spot a bad listing from a mile away: the ones that tried to sell "cozy" as a code for "claustrophobic" and "charming" as a synonym for "you'll be sharing the building with a family of raccoons." I had a list of criteria—things I absolutely needed to survive my next move. Top of the list? A garage. Winters in Minneapolis are nothing to scoff at, and after spending too many mornings scraping ice off a bus stop bench, I was determined never to face the cold without a car and a proper garage to keep it in.

So, when I found an apartment with a garage included, I felt like I'd hit the jackpot. Sure, the rent was a little higher, but it was worth it. The building itself was decent, too— nothing fancy, but the kind of place where you could live quietly without worrying about neighbors throwing impromptu keg parties under your window.

Or so I thought.

The first two years in the new apartment were, dare I say, good. There were a few annoyances here and there— like the kids in the building who seemed to treat the hallway as their personal racetrack—but overall, it was manageable. I had a garage, a car, and, for the most part, my peace of mind.

That all changed in the third year. It's amazing how one person can completely wreck the atmosphere of a place, and in my case, that person was the new building manager. Her name was Denise, and from the moment she took over, it was like watching a slow-motion train wreck.

Denise was the kind of person who seemed to relish in creating chaos. From the way she handled— didn't handle— maintenance issues to the way she argued with tenants over minor inconveniences, it was clear she was not cut out for property management.

My first real encounter with Denise happened about a month after she took over. It had snowed heavily the night before, and like everyone else in the building, I woke up to find my car trapped behind a thick wall of snow. Now, the garages are in a separate building across the street, and while I was no stranger to winter Iather, I expected the plows to come through and clear the street so I could get to my car. This wasn't my first Minneapolis winter, after all. But two days went by, and the street remained untouched.

On the third day, I finally called the office. Denise answered, her voice laced with the kind of annoyance that made me feel like I was already in the wrong for needing help.

Denise sighed; the sound was so heavy it felt like she was physically pushing me away through the phone. "I'll call the plow guy when I get to it. But, you know, snow happens."

It was clear by then that I needed to get out. This wasn't just a bad living situation anymore; it was a slow descent into madness. Thankfully, I managed to find another place before the lease was up, but the exit wasn't without its own set of problems.

The one silver lining? I had a week to move out before the new lease kicked in, so I started transferring my things little by little. But even that wasn't safe from Denise's incompetence—or worse, her dishonesty. One afternoon, while I was at work, she let herself into my apartment and helped herself to a few of my belongings. A couple of small, unimportant things, but still—it was the principle. When I confronted her, she denied everything, naturally.

On the day I finally left for good, I requested a final walk-through, hoping to at least ensure I got my security deposit back without any more drama. But, true to form, Denise refused. She charged me for cleaning, for "stolen" lightbulbs, and for a stove that the cleaning service had left spotless. Pictures didn't matter. Proof didn't matter.

I filed a formal complaint with the company that owned the building. I even took it directly to their office, but they supported Denise in the choices she made. I later learned from other people that this wasn't the first time she had done something like that, but they wished me luck in getting the company to care.

I should've known that wasn't the end. A couple of weeks later, an envelope arrived in the mail with a partial refund of my security deposit. Partial.

According to the itemized list that came with it, I had apparently stolen three lightbulbs from the ceiling fixtures. Lightbulbs. And for this heinous crime, I was being charged $20 apiece. Oh, and there was a $50 cleaning fee for the stove—the same stove that had been scrubbed clean and photographed as evidence.

After everything was said and done, I learned one very important lesson: always, always take pictures of everything before moving out.

### The Thin-Walled Nightmare

After the chaos of Denise and her lightbulb heist, I thought things could only go up from there. And for a brief, shining moment, it seemed like they had. I had found another place that ticked all the right boxes: a two-bedroom apartment at a decent price located in a quiet neighborhood. It even came with a bonus—my new landlord offered to paint my bedroom before I moved in and, in a rare gesture of goodwill, let me pick the color.

The first few days in the new apartment were blissfully uneventful. My boxes were unpacked, the cats were exploring their new domain, and I had a lavender bedroom that felt like a personal sanctuary. I started to believe that maybe, just maybe, my apartment nightmare was finally over. But, as with most things in life, reality soon knocked on my door—or, more accurately, slammed into my ceiling.

I was lounging on my couch one evening, enjoying the quiet for once, when I heard a loud thud from above. At first, I thought nothing of it. Everyone drops something once in a while. But then it happened again. Thud. Thud. Thud. It sounded like someone was conducting a demolition derby right above my head.

My cat shot me a wide-eyed look from the armrest as if to say, "What fresh hell is this?"

I sighed and tried to ignore it. But ignoring the thudding was easier said than done. Within a few days, it became clear that this was not a one-time event. It was the soundtrack to my new life. Whoever lived above me seemed to have a personal vendetta against gravity, constantly dropping what sounded like dumbbells, furniture, or possibly even small children onto the hardwood floors.

And it wasn't just the noise from above. Oh no, that would have been too simple. My next-door neighbors, a couple with a talent for loud arguments, quickly made their presence known. If the thin walls weren't already an issue, their screaming matches ensured that I could hear every insult, every door slam, and every storm-off in full stereo.

It didn't take long before I got to know them more intimately than I ever wanted to. I knew when they were having sex, too, which was quite often.

"I should've been more upfront about the noise issue," the landlord admitted, sounding more apologetic than I had expected. "If I had told you, you probably wouldn't have taken the place."

She wasn't wrong. After some negotiations, I not only went out of the remainder of my lease without penalty, but they also agreed to return my security deposit in full and pay for my moving expenses.

## A Glimmer of Hope – The Community Room Apartment

After escaping the thin-walled nightmare, I was ready for a fresh start. Again. This time, I had my standards. No more paper-thin walls. No more landlords with a questionable grasp of reality. I wanted peace, quiet, and maybe—just maybe—a place I could actually call home for longer than a year.

When I found the next apartment, I thought I might've finally hit the jackpot. It was in a decent neighborhood, the rent was affordable, and best of all, it had a community room. The idea of hosting game nights and holiday dinners again was something I was looking forward to.

The apartment itself was modest but charming in that old-school way and the neighbors seemed friendly enough. I was cautiously optimistic.

Not long after I moved in, I started using the community room regularly. Game nights, dinner parties, you name it. I hosted a holiday dinner for 50 people one year.

It wasn't long before I got into a rhythm. The quiet nights in my own unit were a change from the chaos I'd endured before.

That is until the management changed.

I've come to realize that if there's one constant in apartment living, it's that as soon as things start to get comfortable, something or someone will inevitably throw a wrench in the works. In this case, it was the new manager— the owner's son, Bryan. Bryan had a way of turning minor inconveniences into major problems, mostly by ignoring them until they exploded into something too big to handle.

The first sign of trouble came when the security system on the front door started acting up. It worked perfectly when I moved in, locking behind you with a satisfying click, but one day, it just… stopped. People could walk in and out as they pleased. And walk in they did—strangers, delivery people, even a guy who looked suspiciously like he was just there to enjoy the free warmth of the lobby.

I called Bryan to report the issue, hoping it was just a simple fix, but it took a long time for the problem to be solved.

By the time my lease was up, Bryan and I had come to a mutual understanding: I wouldn't renew, and he wouldn't pretend to care. In a rare moment of professionalism, he actually returned my full security deposit, probably as a way to ensure I wouldn't come back.

## Disappointment in the Next Move

By the time I found my next apartment, I was beginning to think I'd seen it all. Thin walls, bad management, rogue neighbors, and even the occasional refrigerator that sounded like it belonged at an airport runway. How much worse could things really get? I almost didn't want to know.

But when I walked into what would become my new apartment, it felt promising—almost too promising. The property manager, a woman I'll call "Marge," met me at the front door. Marge had that overly friendly, rehearsed tone of someone who'd been showing too many apartments for too many years.

These apartments aren't the traditional type of apartments. They are single-level, single detached units with an attached garage.

I moved in late spring-early summer and discovered that winter that I was expected to shovel my own sidewalks and driveway. They would provide salt for the sidewalks, but I had to go to the office to get it.

It started with the move-in inspection, or rather, the complete lack of one. When I called Marge to schedule it, I got her voicemail. She eventually told me to fill it out and drop it off at the office.

The apartment I got wasn't the apartment I was shown when I did my initial tour. It turns out Marge not only didn't believe in move-in inspections, she apparently didn't do move-out inspections, either. I had the maintenance person to my apartment 23 times in the first two weeks to repair or replace things as I discovered them. My favorite one, though, was when I reported a hole in the garage wall, and the "fix" was to put a plastic mouse trap in front of it to catch critters that might want to come in. For some reason that seemed like a better fix to them than just patching the hole.

But the final straw came when my refrigerator broke. It wasn't an ordinary breakdown, either—it made this horrible grinding noise that could only be described as an airplane engine revving up for takeoff. Every time it kicked on; the entire apartment filled with the sound of mechanical death throes.

Eventually, I did get a new fridge. It arrived one afternoon while I was at work, which meant I had to take off early just to be there for the delivery because Marge refused to enter the apartment to let him in.

By the time my lease was nearing its end, I had lost count of how many times I'd tried to contact Marge. But something amazing happened on move-out day. For the first time in almost a year, I actually got a response. Not a phone call, mind you. No, Marge taped a move-out checklist to my door with clear instructions to leave my keys in the office mailbox when I was done.

There was no final walk-through, no goodbyes, and, predictably, no Marge. However, she did sit in her car on the street and watched me move out. But hey, I got my full security deposit back, which, at that point, felt like a small miracle.

As I drove away from that apartment for the last time, I couldn't help but laugh at how completely absurd the whole experience had been. I'd spent a year chasing down a property manager who might as well have been a ghost, dealing with a refrigerator that sounded like it was plotting its escape, and living with the constant fear that I'd one day wake up to a family of raccoons or mice in my garage.

# Chapter 2

# The Misrepresentation of Senior Living

### False Advertising - The "55+ Community" That Wasn't

By the time I started looking for my next and was hoping to be my last apartment, I was officially over it. The noise, the incompetent management, the never-ending maintenance disasters—it was like a bad soap opera I couldn't escape from. So, when I stumbled across a brand-new building that advertised itself as a 55+ age-restricted community, it felt like a miracle. The thought of living somewhere quiet, where peace and tranquility were practically written into the lease, was too good to pass up.

"No kids," I muttered to myself, scrolling through the listing. "No noise. No chaos. This is it. This is the dream."

It felt like a sign from the universe—a final answer to all my apartment-related prayers. The building was new construction, and moving in meant I was the first one to be living in my apartment. Imagine it: a fresh start in a brand-new unit with no previous occupants to leave behind their noisy ghosts. It was like finding an untouched oasis in the desert of terrible apartment experiences.

I put in my application right away, not minding the long process of paperwork and verifications. After everything I'd been through, what was a few months of waiting?

The day I moved in, I couldn't have been more excited. The building looked pristine, the lobby smelled like fresh paint and new beginnings, and I had a unit on the second floor near the elevator.

And then I started noticing more and more kids in the building. At first, I dismissed it with the thought that they were just visiting their grandparents and then I learned the management hadn't been truthful with me about the nature of the apartment. Despite the advertising, it really wasn't an age-restricted building.

I watched the banner hanging on the building— Welcome to Our 55+ Community—flapping in the wind with bitter irony. Clearly, this was not the age-restricted haven I'd signed up for.

It turned out that when they initially applied for the Section 42 tax credits, the application was for an age-restricted building. However, when the application was denied, they changed the application to the state to say that only one person in the unit had to be 55+. Initially, the state denied that application, but the company filed suit and was eventually awarded the tax credits that allowed children to live in the building.

Things only got worse from there. The building was located right next to a highway, and while they were required to have energy-efficient windows, the building code didn't require any sound abatement measures to be part of the construction.

It was so loud at times that during one phone call with a client, they actually asked me if I was working outside.

The noise was relentless. Given how close the building was to the highway, I asked the county why a sound study wasn't required as a condition of issuing the permit to build. Their response was that they asked the owner to do one, but they couldn't force them to comply.

Road noise studies investigate the impact of vehicle traffic noise on human health, well-being, and the environment. These studies often involve measuring existing noise levels, predicting future noise levels, and identifying ways to mitigate the negative effects of traffic noise, according to the Federal Highway Administration. They can also assess the effectiveness of noise barriers and other noise reduction strategies.

Studies often evaluate the impact of noise on human health and well-being, including stress, sleep disturbance, and annoyance, as well as the potential for noise to affect property values.

In Minnesota, tenants can file a rent escrow action when there is an issue with the property that needs to be addressed. This means instead of paying rent to the landlord, you would pay your rent to the court, and the court would hold it until the issues are resolved. I gave the 30-day notice of my intention to do this, and the management offered to give me noise-canceling headphones and a white-noise machine to help offset the noise issues. This was their way of acknowledging constant loud noise without taking any meaningful long-term measures to solve it.

Fed up with the constant noise, I decided to reach out to the mayor. Maybe if enough people complained, something would be done about the lack of sound abatement measures or at least the highway noise.

I sent an email and, to my surprise, received a response within a few days. But the reply wasn't exactly what I was hoping for.

"Thank you for reaching out," the mayor wrote. "I live just three blocks away from your building, and I can hear the highway from my house, too. Unfortunately, that's just part of living in this area." Perhaps, but where was that information in the advertising? I knew the location of the building, but it never occurred to me that there would be no sound abatement in the building, especially when it was brand new construction. It was a quality-of-life issue that would have prevented me from choosing to move into the apartment in the first place, had I been given the opportunity to make an informed choice.

Two months after moving in, my rent went up by $100. Because it was a Section 42 building, I had to be income-qualified to move into it. That means there is a cap on the amount of income you are allowed to have in order to move in. The amount they charge for rent along with other housing expenses is supposed to be no more than 30% of that income.

The income threshold is based on a calculation using the area median income established by the US Department of Housing and Urban Development. Those guidelines are usually published by March of each year, but because of a government shutdown that year, HUD didn't publish the new AMI rates until June.

My income used to qualify me was based on my March application. When they raised the rent in July, I was now paying more than 30% of my income for housing costs. My landlord tried to make it seem as though HUD was at fault, but the reality is that HUD doesn't provide regulatory oversight to the Section 42 tax credits. The Department of Treasury does. HUD only provides the guidelines for the area median income, and neither one says that rent *had* to be raised just because the AMI rates changed.

And it wasn't just the rent. The building had more than 100 police calls in its first year—drug issues, theft, and even violence.

But the real kicker came when I woke up one morning and discovered my ceiling was full of bugs. At first, I thought it was just a one-off incident—a couple of stray insects that had wandered in. But soon, it became clear that the problem was much bigger. The windows hadn't been sealed properly when the building was constructed.

I wasn't the only one dealing with the bug invasion. Other residents started complaining, too. Some even reported that when it rained outside, it also rained inside their units.

At that point, most of the original tenants—the ones who had moved in hoping for a peaceful, age-restricted community—were already looking for a way out. No one wanted to stick around in a building that clearly was no longer a good place to be.

As if things couldn't get any worse, I soon found out that one of the residents, a retired engineer, was planning to file a lawsuit against the building's owners. Apparently, there were serious structural issues that were causing health problems, and he wasn't about to sit by and watch it happen.

"Good for him," I thought as I began my own search for an attorney. But little did I know, the lawyer I'd eventually hire would take me for an unfortunate ride.

**Impact on Residents**

The emotional impact of realizing that the apartment complex was not the 55+ community it had been advertised as hit hard for many of us. When I first moved in, I had hoped for a peaceful, adult environment where I could connect with like-minded individuals, enjoy quiet moments, and feel safe. It wasn't just an apartment; it was meant to be a place where people like me could begin a new chapter in life, surrounded by others in the same stage. Unfortunately, that expectation was quickly shattered as it became clear that the reality was far different.

The sense of betrayal was palpable among the residents. Many of the residents who had moved in when the building opened were already looking to move out. They hadn't even been there a year, but with the rise in rent, and additional fees for the garage, it was no longer affordable to them, either.

It also wasn't safe. Police were called to the property at least two times a week for things like drugs, theft, and violence.

For me, the emotional toll was significant. It wasn't just about the noise or the false advertising—it was about the people making promises they never intended to keep and wanting me to be ok with that. I didn't want to move anymore. I wanted this to be a place where I'd be able to stay for a long time. It was hard to accept that staying here wasn't going to be a good option for me.

**Psychological Effects**

The ongoing noise and lack of peace were more than just an annoyance; they began to have real psychological consequences. Sleep deprivation became a regular part of life, as it was nearly impossible to get a full night's rest with the constant noise that was coming from outside the building. I started to dread coming home, knowing that my apartment—the one place that was supposed to offer me sanctuary—had become a source of stress and frustration.

Complaints to management went unanswered or were dismissed, leaving us with no recourse but to endure the situation. It felt like I had been deceived, and now I was paying the price—both financially and emotionally.

I wasn't the only one struggling. Other residents spoke of similar feelings of stress and anxiety, with many expressing regret forever moving in.

When we were notified of the rent increase, we were given the option of moving out, if we couldn't afford it. For many of us, it was a catch-22 situation. It's not as though by some miracle we magically had access to more money, but it was going to cost more money to stay and it was going to cost more money to move.

**Raising Concerns / a Quality of Life Issue**

I vividly remember the first time I reached out to the management team about the discrepancies between what was advertised and the reality of our living situation. It started casually enough, with a phone call to the property manager. At first, I naively believed that perhaps the mix-up was just an oversight—maybe someone had slipped through the cracks, or perhaps the management company was in the process of rectifying the situation. After all, I thought, a company that promotes itself as an "expert" in senior housing must surely take tenant complaints seriously.

But that wasn't the case.

In that first phone call, I explained how I, along with other tenants, had moved into the complex under the assumption that it was an age-restricted community.

The main part of the noise issues wasn't so much from inside the building but rather more so from the outside of the building. It was built on a busy highway and there Are no sound abatement measures put in place to mitigate the noise.

Exposure to traffic noise has been associated with a number of illnesses, including cardiovascular disease and diabetes, as well as a range of other health issues, such as stress, annoyance, and sleep disturbance[. According to the WHO, one in three EU citizens is annoyed by environmental noise, and one in four report experiencing sleep disturbance due to this. At an individual level, these non-clinical effects have been suggested to hamper optimal physiological and mental functioning and thus affect quality of life.

I outlined the issues: younger tenants, families with children, and the noise that disrupted what was supposed to be a quiet environment. I expressed my concern that the advertising was misleading and suggested they make changes to ensure that future tenants weren't similarly misled.

This wasn't just a one-off experience. As I began speaking to other residents, I realized that many of us had attempted to raise the same concerns with management, only to be met with similar indifference. One neighbor who had moved into the building for the same reasons I had, described his own attempts to reach out to the management company. He had even written a formal letter detailing how the presence of families with children was making it difficult for him to sleep and enjoy the peaceful retirement he had envisioned. The response he received? A generic, templated letter that essentially reiterated what I had been told—management couldn't (or wouldn't) do anything about it.

## Dismissal of Complaints

As our complaints continued to fall on deaf ears, it became apparent that the management company wasn't just dismissing our concerns—they were actively avoiding responsibility for the misrepresentation. Each time I attempted to raise the issue, the responses became more dismissive.

# Chapter 3

# Seeking Legal Assistance

**Hiring the First Lawyer**

To make any real change, I wanted someone who could navigate the complexities of housing law and tenant rights. The emotional burden of dealing with management's indifference became too much, and the thought of seeking legal counsel, while daunting, offered a potential path to reclaim the peace of mind I had lost.

They had already offered to let me out of my lease, but I wanted something more that would acknowledge the fact that I would not have moved into the building in the first place, had they been truthful with me from the beginning, especially about the part of it not being age restricted.

**The Search for Representation**

Finding a lawyer wasn't an easy task, but it seemed necessary. Minnesota law says that rental housing must be "fit for intended use." The tax credits that were obtained for this building state that the property must be "safe, decent, and affordable." None of that was happening. To date, they are STILL advertising the building as a 55+ building.

Through word of mouth and some recommendations from other residents, I eventually found a lawyer who implied he had experience in dealing with housing disputes and tenant rights violations. I later found out this was nowhere near the truth. During our first consultation, I laid

24

out the facts of the case—the misrepresentation of the building, the influx of younger tenants, and the disturbances that had become part of our daily lives and how it was impacting my health. The lawyer was immediately interested, as he had already represented another tenant in the building. This initial meeting felt like a turning point. After feeling unheard by management, I mistakenly believed I finally found someone who not was going to hold them accountable.

## The First Consultation: Hope for Justice

During the consultation, he took my money for part of his retainer, but he never discussed strategy with me. The rumor in the building was that he got a settlement for the other tenant, although no one knew for sure what that meant. I made the mistake of believing it was something worthwhile. I was tired of all of the nonsense, so I didn't ask a lot of questions.

I later discovered this was another mistake I made. Court records show that the settlement agreement he made for that tenant benefitted the landlord and not the tenant, despite all of the evidence there was in support of the tenant.

He told me he would handle things without providing details of what that meant. He kept insisting that I hired him to get me out of the lease, but that was not true, and even the evidence he provided didn't support that. However, despite not having evidence to support that claim, he never wavered from it.

In addition, he would later say that in that initial meeting, he told me how he handled the tenant's case and I agreed to it. He didn't tell me anything, but if he did, it would have been an ethics violation to discuss someone else's case with me without their knowledge or permission.

If he had been truthful with me, I never would have hired him in the first place.

## Connection to Systemic Issues: Inappropriate Conduct and Betrayal

He didn't have "next steps." He avoided me, argued with me, and pretty much did nothing to advocate for me. I have an email from my landlord telling me she hadn't heard from my attorney and another one from him asking me if I had a different phone number he could call because they aren't returning his calls. If he had just represented another tenant in the building, how did he not know how to contact them? It started the first of many red flags flying for me.

In another email, I asked him why he wasn't advocating for me, and his response was to the effect that he is just a little fish to their big fish. Perhaps, but he knew the size of the pond before he took my case.

Then he sent me a "settlement agreement" he said he negotiated with the landlord that said they would allow me to get out of the remainder of my lease unencumbered if I agreed not to file a suit against them. Wait? What? Long before I hired the attorney, they had already agreed to let me out of the rest of my lease, and there was no supporting evidence to support the claim that getting out of my lease was the reason I involved the attorney in the first place.

When I asked him why it made sense for me to sign away my right to sue, his response was, "Get out first, and I can go after the money later." When I asked how that would be possible if I signed that agreement, I waived my rights to future claims. He refused to answer the question but still insisted I sign it.

I was moving out, regardless of the settlement agreement. I gave notice to my landlord and started to make arrangements to find someplace else. However, the thought of going through this nonsense again with another landlord was making me physically ill, so I chose to look into purchasing a home, and I found a place. He then told my landlord that I needed out of the lease because I purchased a home. Not really. I would have loved to stay in that place if it had been "fit for intended use," as the law requires. I purchased the home because staying in a toxic environment wasn't an option for me – something an attorney who was supposed to be advocating for me should have understood.

I refused to sign the settlement agreement, and he said he would no longer represent me if I refused. I told him by insisting I sign this agreement, and he already wasn't representing me or doing what was in my best interest. They had already agreed to let me out of the lease. I didn't need a settlement agreement that I didn't benefit from to make that part happen. I wanted some sort of financial compensation for being lied to about the nature of the apartment, and he was attempting to make me give that up.

It was the final straw. I had been betrayed by my property managers, by the people who built this so-called community, and now by the very lawyer who was supposed to help me fight back.

As I packed up my things once more, I couldn't help but think back to all the apartments I'd lived in with all the strange, frustrating, and downright ridiculous situations I'd found myself in. There had to be hope somewhere that the next time it would be better.

**Legal Basis for Action: Violations of Minnesota Law**

It was section 42 housing. Section 42 requires the property to be safe, decent, and affordable. The "safe" part went out the window with all of the police calls and the noise issues. Affordable was lost when you had to be income-qualified to move in, and they raised the rent by $100 just two months after I moved in.

Furthermore, Minnesota state law provided additional grounds for my case. The Minnesota Statutes on tenant rights require landlords to maintain fit premises that meet basic standards of habitability, including ensuring quiet enjoyment of the property. The presence of younger tenants who frequently disrupted the peace, along with the constant noise from the highway violated this standard.

My case would also involve management's failure to provide a habitable living environment. According to Minnesota law, landlords are required to address any issues that materially affect the tenant's health, safety, or peaceful enjoyment of the premises. Their inaction in response to the noise complaints and the number of police reports on a regular basis should have made a difference. He never raised these issues with me, even though they were issues that, according to court records, were similar to what the other tenant experienced.

Another legal issue that was never raised in either of my cases was about retaliation. With the other tenant, the management started an eviction process right after he initiated a rent escrow action. However, that was never mentioned in the settlement agreement he was given to sign.

In my situation, my ledger shows my rent was paid in full on time, yet a few days after that, an additional amount was added to my account without notifying me and without a justification for it. This also came after I had given them notice of my intent to file a rent escrow action. I learned about it after receiving a notice that they were intending to initiate an eviction for an outstanding balance on my account. I was going to be evicted for money I didn't owe, but my attorney never raised the issue in my defense.

The complex wasn't truthful about it being an age-restricted property, it wasn't safe, there were construction issues that impacted the quality of life in the building, and it was to be an income-qualified property, yet they raised the rent two months after I moved in, and the best my attorney could do is come up with a settlement agreement that benefitted my landlord.

## I didn't benefit from his representation, my landlord did

I wanted financial compensation. He never explained anything to me. Whenever I would ask a question or what further information, the emails I have show he was either dismissive of me or snarky with me.

I once asked him why he wasn't, at a minimum, asking for money to cover my moving expenses, and he responded that he didn't think a judge would award any of that. If I wasn't going to court, what difference did it make what the judge thought? He wouldn't ask for anything.

I wanted him to negotiate a financial settlement, and he refused. He would later say I tried to force him to ask for $50k and he didn't want to upset them by asking for it. I wanted him to start with that as a negotiating point and see how they would respond, but he wouldn't even ask for moving expenses.

I wanted him to raise the issue of retaliation and he refused. I wanted to go to court, but he didn't want to so he would argue with me or just ignore me. My legal arguments had merit and I supported them with evidence, but he wasn't interested. I wanted what I experienced to be part of a public record, but he kept fighting me on that.

He kept insisting that I hired him to get me out of my lease, but the evidence didn't support that – even his own evidence didn't support that claim. There were a few times when I asked him who he was representing – me or my landlord and all I got was a snarky response or ignored.

He never intended to represent me. This came out later in his suit against me. He doesn't really deny this. He just doesn't think it is wrong. After I fired him, I asked him for a copy of my file. There was nothing in it of any correspondence he had with my landlord. It was mostly the information I had given to him.

# Chapter 4

# Betrayal and Legal Setbacks

### Unjust Enrichment

There was no court case, hearing, or other filing in court against my landlord even though that is what I hired him for in the first place. Although I gave my attorney a great deal of information for him to use in supporting my case, he never did anything with it.

None of his information to me or with my landlord even references housing law. It was a housing case, but he wasn't using housing law to defend me. Court records show the same thing for the other tenant. He had a housing case there, too, but there is no mention of housing law in the defense of that, either.

I have an email from my attorney where he claims he can't do much because he is just a little fish in the pond. Perhaps, but he knew the size of the pond when he took my case, so if he felt he couldn't handle it appropriately, he had an ethical obligation to not take my money in the first place.

I wanted him to negotiate a settlement with my landlord, but he refused to do it. Instead of advocating for substantial compensation to address the emotional and financial damages I had suffered, he seemed eager to settle for nothing that benefitted me. He would later say I insisted on him trying to get $50,000 from my landlord, but the evidence doesn't support that. The emails I have between me and him clearly show I wanted that to be a starting point for negotiating. I fully never expected to get that amount, but my reasoning was that if you start low, the end result will be even lower. Therefore, if you start higher, the end result should be more reasonable.

## Failure to Properly Represent Me or My Interests

My landlord didn't offer anything because my attorney never asked them for anything. It was an issue that came up later in his suit against me that he was unwilling to even try to negotiate for moving expenses. By not even asking for moving expenses and wanting me to waive future claims, he wasn't representing me, even for things that were easy to get.

## Emotional Fallout: Disillusionment with the Legal System

The realization that my lawyer had become yet another obstacle in my fight for justice hit me hard. When I first hired legal counsel, I believed that I had finally found someone who would hold my landlord accountable for its misrepresentation and mismanagement. Instead of providing solutions, the lawyer became part of the problem.

I hired him to represent me with the hope that doing something for me could open the door for other people to benefit from it. But it didn't get there because he made no effort to do the right thing.

In the information I have, he doesn't really even try to deny this. He just argues with me about wanting it to be wrong. In fact, when I asked for my file, there wasn't anything in it of any contact or conversation with my landlord. What he returned to me was nothing more than what I had given to him.

Eventually, he dropped me as a client without warning. I found out through my landlord that he had withdrawn from my case, but he never communicated this to me directly.

I asked him to return the money I paid him, and he refused, so I filed a complaint with the Office of Lawyers Professional Responsibility.

## Complaining to OLPR proved to be useless

*This was the second time he was put on probation.*

I filed a complaint with the Office of Lawyers Professional Responsibility about the way he was handling my case. Multiple times I asked why his lack of evidence didn't seem to matter, and each time there was either no response or a response that didn't make sense.

At the time there were others who had complaints against him and so I was included with them when he was ultimately taken to court to be put on supervised probation. However, despite all of the harm he did to me, all that got included on my behalf in the court hearing was that he didn't give me a receipt for the cash part of his retainer.

I wasn't given an explanation as to why nothing else mattered.

He was eventually put on supervised probation, but his probation agreement didn't include any restitution for anyone he harmed, and OLPR told me to file a claim with the Client Security Board to get my money back. The Client Security Board told me they don't pay when attorney misconduct is involved – something OLPR already knew when they told me to file the claim.

## Small Claims Court Turned Out To Be Useless

The Client Security Board suggested I file a suit in conciliation court, so I did. Throughout this case, he deflected, avoided, made statements that weren't true, and still didn't provide any evidence that he did anything meaningful to represent me.

I won a default judgment after he didn't show up at the final hearing. He would later claim he didn't show up because he never received the notice of the hearing – of all of the notices he got for this and other hearings, this one magically didn't show up.

This wasn't the first time the judge allowed him to use his courtroom as a playground, and it wouldn't be the last.

## The Defamation Suit - *Note that he was on probation when he filed this suit.*

He appealed the judgment and retaliated by filing a defamation suit against me. The initial filing said things that followed a consistent pattern that ended up throughout all of this – it didn't make sense, it wasn't supported with evidence, let alone credible evidence and no one required him to make sense or provide evidence.

It started off with how he was irreparably harmed because I "forced" him to take cash for part of his retainer, yet what he provided as "evidence" didn't support this claim.

He also said he was harmed when I went to the Client Security Board, although nothing resulted from it and he never had to say why or how he was harmed.

It wasn't a probation violation to file a suit that made no sense and wasn't supported by evidence, and the court opened the doors to allow him to play.

He told the court it was my fault that one of the terms of his probation was that he was supposed to tell potential new clients he was on probation. Neither OLPR nor the judge said he was wrong to blame me for that being a part of the probation agreement he agreed to in order to keep his license.

He also told the court that he could file false claims in court because OLPR never told him it was wrong to do so. When I asked the judge how this made sense and why he was allowed to do this, all I got was ignored.

# Chapter 5

# Brian Scott VanMeveren

## Hiring Brian VanMeveren

I hired Brian to hold my landlord accountable. My evidence and to a large degree so does Brian's supports this. He kept telling the court that I hired him to get me out of my lease. None of the evidence – even the evidence he submitted – supports this, yet he never wavered from it.

My landlord had already offered to let me out of my lease, but I wanted something more. I wanted an acknowledgment that I never would have moved into the building had they been truthful from the beginning, especially about it not being an age-restricted property.

Minnesota law states that rental housing must be fit for its intended use. The tax credits obtained for this building require the property to be safe, decent, and affordable. None of that was happening. Even now, they are still advertising the building as a 55-plus residence.

Through word of mouth from other residents, I eventually found Brian. There were other tenants who were hopeful because if things worked out for me as well as what they heard he did for one other tenant, they wanted to hire him, too.

Rumor had it he reached a settlement for the other tenant, although no one knew exactly what that entailed. I made the mistake of assuming it was worthwhile.

During our first consultation, he never discussed strategy with me, and he never denied avoiding it. He just acted like it was unnecessary. I was exhausted from all the nonsense, so I didn't ask many questions. I thought I had finally found someone who would hold my landlord accountable. I was wrong.

Later, I discovered another mistake. Court records showed that the settlement he arranged benefitted the landlord, not the tenant, despite the significant evidence supporting the tenant's claims.

He told me he would handle things but never explained what that meant. When I would ask questions, he would either talk down to me or ignore what I was asking altogether.

He later claimed that during our first meeting, he had explained how he handled the previous tenant's case and that I agreed to it. He did not tell me anything. Even if he had, it would have been an ethics violation to discuss another client's case without their knowledge or consent.

Had he been truthful with me, I never would have hired him.

He admitted to an ethics violation to cover up a lie, and this wasn't a probation violation, nor did the court find anything wrong with it.

## Systemic Issues Continue

He had no plan for the next steps. He avoided me, argued with me, and failed to advocate for me. I have an email from my landlord stating she had not heard from my attorney, and another email from him asking if I had a different phone number because they were not returning his calls. If he had recently represented a tenant in the same building, how could he not know how to contact them? That was the first of many red flags.

In another email, I asked him why he was not advocating for me. He responded by saying he was just a small fish in comparison to their big fish. Perhaps that was true, but he knew the size of the pond when he took my case.

He eventually sent me a settlement agreement he claimed to have negotiated with the landlord. It said they would let me out of the rest of my lease if I agreed not to file a lawsuit. But they had already offered to let me out before I hired him, so I didn't need an agreement to be let out of the lease.

When I asked him why I should sign away my right to sue, his response was to get out first and then go after the money. When I pointed out that signing the agreement would waive my future claims, he refused to answer and still insisted I sign.

I refused, and he told me he would no longer represent me. I told him he already was not representing me by trying to push an agreement that offered me no benefit. I did not need his help to be released from the lease. I wanted financial compensation for being lied to about the nature of the apartment. He was trying to make me give that up.

That was the final straw. I had been betrayed by my property managers, by the people who built this so-called community, and now by the lawyer who was supposed to help me fight back.

## Legal Basis for Action: Violations of Federal and State Law

This was Section 42 housing. Section 42 mandates that properties be safe, decent, and affordable. Safety was compromised by constant police presence and noise issues. Affordability was questionable since the rent was raised by one hundred dollars just two months after I moved in, despite income qualification requirements.

Minnesota state law offered even more support for my case. It requires landlords to maintain habitable premises and uphold the tenant's right to quiet enjoyment.

The property was not age-restricted as claimed. It was not safe. There were construction issues that disrupted the quality of life. It was supposed to be income-qualified, yet rent was increased soon after I moved in. And the best my attorney could come up with was a settlement agreement that protected the landlord.

I wanted financial compensation. He never explained anything to me. Whenever I asked questions, his responses were dismissive or sarcastic.

At one point, I asked why he was not at least negotiating for my moving expenses. He said a judge probably would not award it. But if I was not going to court, what did a judge's opinion matter? He still would not ask.

I asked him to negotiate a financial settlement. He refused. He later claimed I tried to force him to demand fifty thousand dollars and that he did not want to upset them. I wanted it as a starting point, a negotiation tactic. He would not even ask for moving costs.

I asked him to bring up retaliation. He refused. I said I wanted to go to court. He argued with me or ignored me. My legal arguments had merit and were backed by evidence. He did not care. I wanted the record public. He pushed back on that too.

I asked him more than once who he was representing—me or my landlord. I got sarcasm or silence in return.

He never truly intended to represent me. That came out later in his suit against me. He did not deny it. He just did not think it was wrong.

After I fired him, I asked for a copy of my file. There was no correspondence with the landlord. The file only contained the information I had provided to him. In the very least, it should have contained logs or some other evidence of his contacts with my landlord, but it didn't. Which begs the question that if he had evidence of advocating for me, as he kept insisting he did, why wouldn't he want to prove it to me?

## Brian VanMeveren's Probation

When Brian filed a defamation suit against me in retaliation for the small claims suit I filed, he was already on probation. Yet it was not a violation of his probation to file claims that lacked substance or supporting evidence.

He even argued that I was the cause of his probation, despite it being a direct result of his own actions. He claimed that holding him accountable would somehow harm him.

That alone shows how broken the system is when a probation agreement holds no real weight.

There is no real substance in how the probation agreement is written. There are no consequences for failing to follow or meet its terms. It says he must comply with the rules of professional conduct, yet even with clear evidence that he did not, nothing was considered a violation. It felt like a slap in the face to everyone he had harmed.

## What the Probation Agreement Says

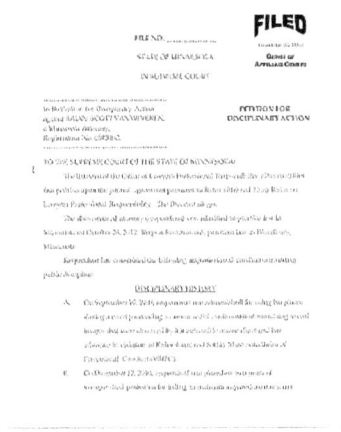

*Official court filing below: Petition for Disciplinary Action filed November 23, 2020*

## The Text of the Probation Agreement:

## Disciplinary Action Against Brian Scott VanMeveren

The official petition for disciplinary action highlights Brian's troubling record. He had been licensed since 2012 but faced serious issues handling a legal matter for a client named L.L., a mother who needed his help appealing the termination of her parental rights.

In January 2020, L.L. hired Brian to file a petition with the Minnesota Supreme Court. They agreed on a flat fee of fifteen thousand dollars, and she paid ninety-five hundred upfront. Brian assumed he had thirty days to file. He failed to check the correct legal rules. The real deadline was fifteen days. He filed on January twenty-ninth. The court rejected it. He then filed a motion asking for a late acceptance and blamed a misunderstanding of the rules. The Supreme Court denied it on February 3rd.

Instead of accepting responsibility, he shifted the blame to L.L., saying she had not provided documents on time, even though it was his responsibility to know the law and meet deadlines.

On June 7, 2021, the Minnesota Supreme Court conditionally reinstated him following a suspension for professional misconduct. The April 27 order that year had suspended him for at least thirty days due to those violations. To return, he had to comply with the Minnesota Rules of Professional Conduct and pass the Multistate Professional Responsibility Examination.

*Official reinstatement order filed June 7, 2021*

After the suspension, Brian submitted an affidavit claiming he met the terms except for passing the MPRE. The Office of Lawyers Professional Responsibility did not oppose his reinstatement, provided he agreed to additional terms. He was reinstated on June 10, 2021, and placed on a two-year probation.

During this time, he was required to fully cooperate with OLPR monitoring, respond promptly to correspondence, and notify them of any contact changes. He had to work under a supervising attorney, submit monthly inventories of client files, and maintain ethical standards.

He also had to establish office procedures that ensured timely responses and proper handling of legal matters. He was required to pass the MPRE by April 27, 2022. Failure to do so would trigger an automatic suspension.

This order was meant to balance accountability with an opportunity for rehabilitation. It stressed the importance of ethical conduct in preserving public trust in the legal profession. His reinstatement aimed to provide a structured return to practice while protecting his clients and the public.

**Where it Failed**

Brian's probation agreement required him to be supervised and submit monthly reports. I asked where was the evidence that he was actually complying with this term of his probation, and it was another question that got ignored, as well as another place where evidence wasn't required to support his claims.

Yet, in court, he claimed that informing potential clients about his probation status had harmed his practice and it was my fault he was supposed to tell potential clients about his probation. As a solo practitioner, how viable could his business have been if he had actually disclosed this for two full years?

However, the thing to note in the entire court proceedings is that he just blamed me for his probation. Not his own choices in his conduct or the other people he harmed. Just me.

I raised the issue with both OLPR and with the court that if he is a victim of his own making and unable or unwilling to be accountable for his own conduct, then why is he allowed to have a license in the first place, but to no one's real surprise, I never got an answer from anyone.

"Restoring the public trust" and "protecting his clients" was nothing but an empty soundbite that had no substance to it, and the court said this was how it was supposed to work.

# Chapter 6

# Tim Maher

## Betrayal by Tim Maher

Brian used the court to retaliate against me and the judge allowed him to use his courtroom as a playground to do it. When it became clear that the judge was going to allow Brian to continue without evidence and to a large degree without even making sense, I felt that if I was to get off this merry-go-round, it would be necessary for me to hire an attorney to help get me there.

I thought I was doing well with the first attorney I hired until I showed up for a hearing and he wasn't able to answer the judge's questions about why I was there. He looked like a deer caught in headlights.

After the hearing, he stopped communicating with me. When I went to the partner of the law firm, he told me he would be willing to take over the case if I came up with a $15,000 retainer for him. He wasn't bothered that the lawyer who worked for him had abandoned my case, so it was difficult for me to put that kind of trust in him to do the right thing for me.

So, I fired them and went in search of another attorney I was hoping would finally completely end all of this nonsense. I got a referral for Tim Maher.

At first, things seemed to be going well. That changed on June 12, 2023, when I realized he had been deceiving me all along.

The June 12 hearing was part of the lawsuit Brian had filed against me. According to what Tim had told me, it was supposed to be a day for Brian to answer for fraud, unjust enrichment, and breach of contract.

The hearing was supposed to bring attention to the serious charges against Brian. The fact that the court had allowed the matter to proceed suggested to me that my case had merit. Yet what actually happened in the courtroom was nothing short of an unfortunate scam, orchestrated by Tim and Brian's attorney, and supported by the judge.

## Secret Meetings and Lack of Transparency

When I arrived at the courthouse, I expected to face Brian's claims and tell my side of the story. But as soon as I arrived, Tim and Brian's attorney disappeared into the judge's chambers. I had no idea why they went in or what they were doing. Just a week earlier, I visited Tim's office where we discussed the trial strategy. I was fully prepared for trial and had no reason to believe anything else was going to happen. But without my knowledge or consent, Brian's attorney and Tim had colluded together on a settlement arrangement and entered chambers to present it to the judge.

Meanwhile, I sat in the courtroom across from Brian, completely unaware of what they were doing to me.

While Brian's attorney and Tim were in the chambers, Brian threatened me. I later filed a police report, but the judge dismissed it, as he would go on to do with so many other things. When they returned and announced a "settlement arrangement," I was blindsided. I had never been

48

told anything about a deal. I had not agreed to one. I had no knowledge that any negotiations had even taken place. To make it worse, the arrangement was never put in writing.

It was a settlement arrangement that made no sense.

Tim thought he would get away with ambushing me with the execution of it. The arrangement he made was that Brian would read three sentences to me – sentences that Tim wrote – that made no sense, didn't include an apology, and didn't require Brian to own his conduct. His plan was to have me meet him in the hallway outside the courtroom without telling me Brian and his attorney would be there, and Brian would read the sentences to me, thereby fulfilling the execution of the arrangement.

However, it backfired because I wasn't aware I was supposed to stay after the hearing and I left, while they waited in the hallway for me to show up. When they realized I had left, Tim tried to make other arrangements for me to let Brian do this to me. He wanted me to set up another time to go back to the courthouse or set an appointment to go to Brian's office. When I realized what he was doing, I refused to agree to go along with it.

What he wanted Brian to do to me was not only abusive, it was wrong. Brian could lie to me, treat me like crap, and get rewarded for it. Tim was supposed to be MY attorney, yet he made arrangements for me to be abused and got to use the court to do it.

I have the transcript from the hearing. It does not specify what the arrangement actually was (I refuse to call it an agreement because there never was any on my part). The judge merely asked if I agreed to "this," without clarifying what "this" meant. I said yes, but only out of fear. Brian had just threatened me, and in that moment, I realized Tim had betrayed me.

The thing to note is that when the judge spoke without giving details or clarification on the details or terms of this arrangement, Tim was silent. There is nothing in the court records that provides evidence of him asking for it to be fully entered into the court records. If he was my attorney and the arrangement was for my benefit, it would seem that he would want it to be part of the record so that if Brian deviated from it, there would be a way to hold him accountable. However, as it turned out, this arrangement wasn't for my benefit. Tim did it for Brian's benefit, even though Tim was supposed to be my lawyer.

When I later tried to challenge the arrangement, the judge told me I should have spoken up at the time. But I had just been threatened, and I was still trying to process the fact that my own lawyer had lied to me. I did not feel safe or supported by the court.

The judge also said the records would be sealed, as part of the arrangement Tim and Brian's lawyer had made. I had come for a trial. I wanted everything on the public record. But once again, something happened behind closed doors that robbed me of that right.

As I stood in court listening to terms I had never would have agreed to, had it even been discussed with me, I felt as if I had been dropped into a surreal nightmare. Everyone around me was operating by secret rules while I was kept in the dark and expected to go along. The very system I had turned to for justice now felt like a carefully orchestrated trap.

## Allegations of Misconduct and Blackmail

After firing Tim, I filed a motion to dismiss the settlement arrangement. In response, I received an email from Tim that I saw as an attempt to blackmail me into dropping that motion.

Tim's email only deepened the betrayal I already felt. He pushed me to accept the deal despite never putting it in writing or explaining why he had negotiated terms that allowed Brian to continue harming me. He acted as though I had no real choice. He expected me to accept something that felt as fraudulent as the behavior I had originally accused Brian of.

I gave that email to the judge, hoping it would support my claim that I had never agreed to any arrangement. The judge ignored it, just as he ignored everything else that should have mattered.

I also told the judge that if Tim really did have evidence that he discussed this arrangement with me and I agreed to it, all Tim would have to do is provide it, but Tim couldn't provide it because it didn't exist.

However, the had to be some kind of documentation of communication between Tim and Brian's attorney where they discussed this arrangement and how it would be implemented, yet both sides refused to provide it and the judge never required them to produce it.

If Brian's attorney felt Tim didn't make this arrangement in good faith, she could have produced the documentation to support her claim, but instead, she avoided the issue altogether and the judge allowed it to happen.

This was yet another time when the lawyer I hired to represent me failed to act in my best interests. Like Brian before him, Tim took my money and threw me under the bus. And just like before, the judge supported it.

Tim was not truthful with me. He was working for Brian's benefit. He often talked about Brian apologizing to me, but Brian had no intention of doing that. Tim even wrote the statements Brian was supposed to read to me and then tried to force me through the process.

Before the hearing, I had met with Tim in his office. There were witnesses present who can confirm that everything we discussed was about preparing for trial. At no point did Tim bring up any settlement arrangement. He avoided the topic, danced around it, and never once used the word "settlement." He briefly mentioned an amount of five thousand dollars, but when we got to court, that was reduced to three thousand. He never explained what the money was for or what it related to. I was never given a chance to oppose the deal because I was never told it existed.

Even beyond that, the arrangement itself made no sense. There was nothing in writing. No evidence. The judge kept giving them room to bend the rules. I later learned that Tim had written three sentences for Brian to read aloud, and in exchange for this performance, I was expected to agree to seal the records. It was not an apology. It was not sincere. It was not something Brian had to mean. When I asked the judge how it made sense for Brian to treat me terribly and then be rewarded for it, I was met with silence.

There is still nothing in writing. If this had been a legitimate settlement, I would have something to show that I had agreed to it. But there is nothing in the transcript that defines what the arrangement was. I do, however, have an email from Tim that I believe was a veiled attempt at blackmail to keep me from challenging the arrangement.

Tim told me that the OLPR said he was allowed to do this. Later, OLPR claimed it was just a case of "sloppy representation." But Tim was not inexperienced. He knew exactly what he was doing. He lied to the court and wanted me to accept it all for Brian's benefit.

Tim was supposed to be my lawyer. Yet the arrangement he made gave me nothing. He created an opportunity for Brian to hurt me again and tried to push me into it. He essentially signed my name to a deal I never saw and denied me the ability to choose between trial and settlement. His actions left me with no control over my own legal defense.

If he had legitimate evidence that I knew about and agreed to the arrangement, none of this would have been necessary. And if he was really representing me, why would he ever agree to a deal that harmed me? He was the one who wrote those insulting statements for Brian. He wanted me to reward Brian for harming me.

I asked repeatedly how any of this made sense. No one had an answer.

I also raised concerns about the vague language in the deal, particularly the use of the term "disparagement," which seemed deliberately unclear. Brian's original claim had been defamation, so how and when did that switch to disparagement? No one was willing to answer.

To me, this only proved what I already believed. Brian could not prove defamation, so he found another way to retaliate, and Tim helped him do it.

I asked the judge why Tim's not being truthful with me or with him did not matter and why it didn't matter that Tim was not able to provide evidence to support his claims.

It was yet another time when the judge chose to ignore me and the issues I was raising.

Eventually, I terminated Tim Maher's services. I filed a motion to vacate the settlement, pointing to the lack of informed consent and the misconduct involved.

*See above the email Tim Maher sent me on June 29, 2023,
following my motion to vacate the settlement arrangement.*

Tim's response was to send me an email stating that because I had fired him, our communications were no longer protected by attorney-client privilege. He acknowledged that Brian's attorney had told him about my motion. He said the Rules of Professional Conduct allowed him, though did not require him, to respond and reveal our communications. He said he had not decided yet if he would respond, but warned me to consider withdrawing my motion if I did not want him to disclose anything.

If he had evidence that I discussed and agreed to a settlement, the blackmail would not have been necessary. I would have had something to show the court. But there was nothing.

# Chapter 7

# OLPR

## (Office of Lawyers Professional Responsibility)

### Problems with OLPR

The Office of Lawyers Professional Responsibility is the licensing agency for attorneys. It is also supposed to be the place that holds attorneys accountable for their conduct.

In 2021, staff from that office wrote to Minnesota Supreme Court Justice Natalie Hudson and asked her to remove the Executive Director from her position due to how the office had been handling and mishandling cases. Justice Hudson not only refused to take action but also declined to require any changes in how the office operated.

The problems in the office continue and it is those who are harmed by attorney misconduct that are most impacted by it.

The Minnesota State Bar Association describes ongoing problems with OLPR in a blog on their website.[1]

For the second time in a decade, the Office of Lawyers Professional Responsibility (OLPR) is in substantial violation of its legal duty to process ethics complaints

---

[1] Wernz, W. (2025, February 6). OLPR is again missing its priority goal of prompt complaint dispositions by a mile. https://mnbars.org/?pg=legal_ethics&commpg

promptly. A recent Lawyers Board filing in the Supreme Court stated, "The Board's concern lies. . .in the indisputable fact that OLPR decisions routinely take, by any measure, too long."[i] OLPR's Director was appointed nine years ago to rectify a similar problem, but – after initially identifying OLPR's file-aging problem as the "number one priority" – the Director's writings now generally ignore the problem and claim, implausibly, that the problem is insoluble or requires substantial staff additions to solve.

Promptness is "primary" for several reasons. Lawyers who have engaged in serious misconduct should not be held out to an unsuspecting public as trustworthy. Lawyers who have erred in minor ways need correction. The public should have its complaints addressed promptly. File-aging and file-closing statistics are important indicators of OLPR's efficiency and productivity. This can be further seen on their official website https://mnbars.org/.

In my lawsuit against Brian to recover my money, I submitted more than sixty pages raising the question, "Where is his evidence?" Yet when OLPR took him to court, the only issue they addressed was that he had failed to give me a receipt for his retainer.

Brian was on probation when he retaliated by filing a lawsuit against me, claiming he was "irreparably harmed" because I "forced" him to take cash. The document he submitted in support of that claim did not actually support it, but filing false claims apparently is not considered a probation violation.

I provided them with the email from Tim Maher's veiled attempt to blackmail me into not challenging the settlement arrangement. OLPR's response was to call it "sloppy representation." When I asked if they had any process to ensure that "sloppy representation" would not happen to anyone else, I was ignored.

Tim intentionally and deliberately lied to the court when he made the settlement arrangement that benefited Brian without my knowledge or consent. That, too, was not considered a problem by OLPR. In fact, at one point, Tim even claimed that OLPR supported him in doing that to me.

**Responses That Do Not Make Sense**

One letter from OLPR claimed that my complaint against the judge had been forwarded to the Judicial Review Committee because OLPR does not handle complaints against judges.

That would have made sense if I had actually asked them to investigate the judge, but I had not. My request was clear: I wanted my concerns about the judge included in my ongoing complaints against Brian's attorney, Tim Maher, and Brian VanMeveren.

I had already clarified this in an email exchange with Joseph Ambroson, a court official who assured me that my emails would be added to my file. So why was OLPR now misrepresenting what I had said? It felt as if they had not even read my communications. The mishandling of my complaint was more than a simple oversight—it was evidence that they were not listening. How could the system hope to fix anything if it could not even get the basics right?

Another response from OLPR was equally troubling. It excused the conduct of Brian's attorney—even though she signed off on Brian's motions and argued that holding him accountable "hurt his feelings"—on the grounds that I had failed to respond to correspondence in December.

To be clear, I did not respond because there was nothing to respond to. I never received any letters, calls, or emails. How was I supposed to reply to silence? OLPR complaints are usually assigned to an investigator. Who was the investigator in my case?

"If we were in kindergarten, perhaps that would be acceptable," I wrote in my response. "But even kindergartners are required to correct their behavior to prevent harm to others."

Despite the clear evidence of unethical actions, my complaints were dismissed. OLPR refused to recognize their misconduct for what it was—even though the Rules of Professional Conduct explicitly condemn such behavior.

**Fighting for Accountability**

What frustrates me the most is that this is not just about me—it is about the integrity of the legal system itself.

"Lying to the court is wrong," I wrote in one of many emails. "It even says so in the Rules of Professional Conduct."

Yet Brian and his attorney acted as if those rules did not apply to them. Brian even filed a motion claiming it was permissible to submit false claims in court because OLPR had not explicitly told him he could not.

I could not stay silent. I challenged OLPR to justify their actions—or their lack of action.

*Attached below: Full version of my detailed follow-up email to OLPR officials, outlining contradictions in their process*

"Instead of excuses and other nonsense," I wrote, "in your next letter, show some integrity and offer a justification for your belief that it is acceptable for attorneys to purposely and intentionally lie to a judge. The state statute says it is wrong, so please tell me where your authority comes from to say that the law does not matter when it comes to acceptable standards of conduct for attorneys."

This is not just about my case. It is about principle. If lawyers cannot be held accountable for basic honesty and integrity, then what hope is there for justice?

## Correspondence with OLPR Officials

I emailed Joseph Ambroson (he was the "investigator" assigned to the complaint I filed on Brian) on Thursday, May 23, to express my frustration with how Brian VanMeveren has continued to act without consequences despite the lies, threats, and unethical conduct.

*See above: Email message I sent to OLPR official Joseph Ambroson on May 23, 2024.*

I addressed Joseph directly, asking how his office could still support Brian after everything—after lying in court, committing fraud, and submitting false claims without evidence.

I pointed out that Rule 11 of the Minnesota Rules of Civil Procedure is supposed to hold people accountable for filing lawsuits with false or malicious intent. Yet Brian faced no repercussions. He even admitted in court that he could file false claims without fear of consequences because OLPR had not stopped him. I made it clear that even though the case was closed and I could not change the decision, Brian's conduct throughout the process still mattered and should not be excused.

*(See above: My email to Joseph Ambroson on May 24, 2024, referencing Minnesota Rule 11 and outlining how Brian violated it without facing consequences.)*

I highlighted several specific actions: Brian falsely accused me of forcing him to take cash for his retainer. He filed claims with no supporting evidence. He threatened me in the courtroom. I reminded Joseph that I had to file a police report due to Brian's threats, yet his office had ignored it. I also told him how the judge had discouraged me from filing an ethics complaint against Brian, which had further impaired my ability to protect myself.

Finally, I expressed my anger that Brian still holds his law license and has been rewarded for lying, threatening, and harassing me. I urged Joseph to at least acknowledge that this behavior is wrong and that allowing Brian to continue practicing law is a failure of integrity.

In his response, Joseph Ambroson acknowledged my frustration with both the court cases and OLPR. He confirmed that he had received my emails and was treating them as replies to his earlier letter dated May 22, 2024, which requested additional information.

He reiterated that OLPR cannot overturn any court decisions, something I already knew. He also noted that the office had already reviewed some of the issues I raised and therefore could not reconsider them. However, he said they were still investigating whether Brian had violated any rules of professional conduct and that my responses would assist that investigation. He asked if I had any further questions related to the current complaint.

I wasn't asking him to overturn any court decisions. The court hadn't made any decisions at that point to be overturned. Brian was using the court as his playground – while he was on probation, and they made it clear that what he was doing wasn't a probation violation, nor was it a violation of professional conduct to submit false claims to the court.

In other words, he acknowledged my concerns but reminded me that OLPR could only address the specific issues they had chosen to investigate and could not revisit previous matters.

But what part of this is "going back?"

They never ruled on anything to begin with. There never was an investigation.

*See below: Letter I wrote detailing the court's refusal to let me defend myself or file ethics*

If Brian had simply produced evidence showing I hired him to get out of my lease, this entire situation could have been resolved long ago.

## OLPR's Failure Is Well Documented

The purpose of OLPR is to oversee attorney conduct. Yet their failure to fulfill this responsibility is not just evident in my case—it is confirmed by other sources before I ever came along, as well.

In a letter dated January 31, 2022, the staff of OLPR wrote to Justice Natalie Hudson of the Minnesota Supreme Court requesting the removal of the Director due to poor management and mishandling of cases.

This letter was sent by the Lawyers Professional Responsibility Board in accordance with Rule 5 of the Rules on Lawyers Professional Responsibility. This rule requires the board to provide a recommendation on whether the Director, Susan Humiston, should be reappointed. Their recommendation would guide the Supreme Court's decision.

The board stated that their letter reflected careful deliberation, a review of performance metrics, and input from the public, lawyers, and their own observations.

Although they acknowledged Humiston's legal knowledge and skill, the board unanimously agreed that this did not translate into effective leadership or management. They expressed concern over her failure to deliver on two long-overdue projects: a revised panel manual and a training manual for board members. Despite receiving drafts in early 2021, she missed repeated deadlines and offered only vague explanations and excuses.

The board also criticized her inability to delegate tasks. She claimed she personally handled nearly all aspects of the office's work, from reviewing hundreds of cases to participating in moot court events. Board members found this implausible and unsustainable, suggesting poor management and a lack of confidence in her staff. This led to delays in processing cases and caused harm to both lawyers and complainants. Even during the slowdown caused by the COVID-19 pandemic, when the office had an opportunity to reduce backlogs, no meaningful progress was made.

The quality of OLPR's output was also questioned. Files frequently lacked adequate fact investigation, and analysis of key legal questions, and often contained numerous grammatical and typographical errors. These issues were particularly troubling since the Director claimed to personally oversee every file.

Perhaps most concerning was the Director's defensiveness and lack of accountability. She frequently deflected criticism and blamed others. This unwillingness to take responsibility, combined with the office's dysfunction, led the board to conclude that she lacked the leadership qualities required for the role.

Ultimately, the board recommended that the Director not be reappointed. They based their recommendation on a commitment to accountability, fairness, and professional integrity. The board emphasized the need for leadership that supports collaboration, meets deadlines, and accepts responsibility. These were qualities they believed were absent in her tenure.

Justice Hudson chose not to act on their recommendation. Her inaction sent a message that she supported the ongoing dysfunction, regardless of the harm it caused to those affected by the Director's conduct, and the 2025 blog post on the Minnesota State Bar Association's website is evidence that there was no plan in place for accountability for the office, either.

# Chapter 8

# Judge Patrick Diamond

### Failure of Judicial Conduct

The judge presiding over the small claims case I had against Brian and the case he filed against me was the same judge: Honorable Patrick C. Diamond.

In both cases, he didn't require Brian to present meaningful evidence to support his claims and chose to not respond to any of my motions. I recognize that he couldn't have forced anyone to provide evidence, but he also still chose to support their claims without it.

I asked the judge why I was being held to a higher standard of conduct than the attorneys were, and true to form, he ignored me.

After his final ruling, I filed an ethics complaint with the Board of Judicial Standards. To no one's real surprise, all I got was a pat on the head and essentially told what he did was how courts are supposed to work.

### The Content of the Complaint to the Board of Judicial Standards:

I have faced consistent bias and injustice throughout the court process during the entire time he has been involved. His actions have not only caused harm to me but have also enabled the plaintiff to use the court system to perpetuate further harm. As a woman and, at times, an unrepresented party, I believe his bias against me has been prejudicial to the administration of justice.

There are several serious issues with how he handled my case. First, Judge Diamond does not hold any of the attorneys involved accountable. He does not require them to provide evidence to support their claims, and he does not ensure that they are being truthful. Each time I raised the issue of missing supporting evidence, he would ignore me and allow their claims to stand without it.

For example, when Brian said it was my fault he was on probation and that one of the terms of his probation was that he was required to inform potential clients about it, the judge never questioned it. There were other people Brian harmed that resulted in his probation, yet he denied responsibility for his own conduct. Still, they supported this victimhood narrative and agreed with him that not only was he harmed, but that it was entirely my fault.

He ruled that there was enough evidence for the plaintiff to go to trial on charges that included fraud and unjust enrichment. At that point, I expected a clear and transparent process.

**Secret Meetings and the June 12, 2023 Hearing**

However, on the day of the hearing, there was a secret meeting in his chambers. He returned to the courtroom and announced that a settlement arrangement had been made. While Tim and Brian's attorney were in chambers discussing this arrangement, I was left sitting across the table from Brian. Brian knows how the courts operate. Nothing is recorded unless the judge is present, and he used this opportunity to threaten me about rejecting an arrangement I had no knowledge was even happening. I later filed a police report, but the judge chose to ignore it.

Judicial conduct rules require him to report such threats to the Office of Lawyers Professional Responsibility, but he chose not to report it to them.

There was nothing in writing and nothing in the court transcript that described the full terms and conditions of the arrangement. What I later learned about it made no sense. The judge did not care either. In the transcript, he asked me if I agreed to "this," but never clarified what "this" actually meant. My attorney said nothing about the missing details. That was the moment I realized I had been blindsided and ambushed. The courtroom, which should have been a place of safety and fairness, was not. I responded out of fear, not out of agreement.

I have the transcript. It is clear that the terms of this arrangement are not in it. I included this in the judicial ethics complaint I filed against him, but that led nowhere.

**Bias and Punishment for Seeking Accountability**

I asked for clarification on why he did not require the plaintiff to provide evidence, and he refused to respond.

Another disturbing issue is how he punished me for filing complaints with the Office of Lawyers Professional Responsibility against the attorneys involved in my case. He had previously suggested I file these complaints, yet later used that very action against me. He denied my request to submit the June 12, 2023 transcript to OLPR and even refused to send it directly to the investigator. By withholding this information, he became complicit in the ongoing harm against me. Everything I submitted to OLPR was already part of the court record, so his refusal makes no sense.

Throughout the proceedings, Judge Diamond has shown a clear pattern of bias. He never required the plaintiff to support his claims with evidence. In fact, the plaintiff filed multiple frivolous and unsubstantiated motions, yet the judge allowed them to proceed. In one instance, the plaintiff submitted a motion claiming he did not need to be truthful in court because OLPR had not prohibited it. Judge Diamond allowed this motion to stand. When I filed a motion seeking clarification about the plaintiff's lack of evidence, the court took my filing fee but never responded. This refusal to address my legitimate concerns highlighted the judge's bias against me.

I submitted evidence on multiple occasions that I had been bullied and blackmailed into the settlement arrangement. The June 12 transcript does not reflect whether I had been coerced. Judge Diamond dismissed my concerns. He acknowledged in court that threats had been made against me, yet took no action to address or prevent the resulting harm. Instead, he enforced a settlement that caused me harm and lacked any evidence of my consent. When I asked for an explanation, I received nothing.

His ongoing refusal to demand evidence from the plaintiff, while dismissing mine, reveals a clear imbalance.

The plaintiff was allowed to claim harm from things like contacting the Client Security Board, yet was never asked to provide proof. The judge ignored my motions, refused to justify his rulings, and punished me for seeking protection. When I requested a harassment restraining order after being threatened in court, he interpreted the referee's decision not to grant it as proof that my concerns were baseless. This was a deliberate misrepresentation of the facts and further showed his unwillingness to uphold a fair process.

Moreover, Judge Diamond was aware of misconduct by both the plaintiff and my former attorney. He knew about the blackmail attempts and threats against me and still chose to take no action. His refusal to report this misconduct to OLPR and his unwillingness to acknowledge its impact shows a clear lack of impartiality. Instead, he punished me for defending myself, even though I was fully within my rights to file complaints.

His actions were not just disappointing—they were damaging. He enforced a settlement I did not agree to, failed to protect me when I was threatened in court, and refused to provide transparency or justification for his rulings. His decisions consistently favored a party that admitted to lying and punished me when I sought accountability.

In summary, Judge Diamond has shown a repeated and serious bias. He has refused to require the plaintiff to substantiate his claims. He has ignored my evidence. He has sealed court records without cause. He has punished me for filing valid complaints. His rulings have supported a plaintiff who admitted to dishonesty in court and failed to address misconduct when it mattered most. The personal and legal harm I have endured as a result of his conduct cannot be overstated. His failure undermines public trust in the judicial system.

# Chapter 9

# Systemic Failure: How Each Party Contributed

Brian misled me from the beginning. When he took me on as his client, he never disclosed his lack of experience in housing law. He wasn't upfront about his capabilities, and by his own statements and actions, it's evident that he never had any intention of providing meaningful legal representation. Instead of advocating for me, as he was hired to do, he took my money while my landlord ultimately reaped the benefits.

Brian also misled the Office of Lawyers Professional Responsibility (OLPR). Initially, he told them he had provided me with a receipt for the cash portion of his retainer. OLPR was ready to accept his word and let the matter drop—until I specifically asked them to request the receipt from him. Despite this clear misrepresentation, Brian was never held accountable for lying to me, to them, or to the court. I submitted 65 pages questioning the lack of evidence supporting his claims., yet the only consequence he faced was a minor reprimand for failing to provide a receipt.

In the second case—where Brian sued me—he once again wasn't truthful to me, to OLPR, and to the court. He presented no evidence to support his claims, yet he still benefited from the legal system's inaction. OLPR did not consider his repeated dishonesty a probation violation, and the judge allowed him to proceed without requiring any factual basis for his allegations.

Tim, too, was not truthful, not just with me, but also with OLPR and the court. He falsely represented the existence and nature of a settlement agreement, despite having no evidence to support it. The court records, my personal records with Tim—none of them contain any indication that I was aware of, let alone agreed to, a settlement arrangement that made no logical sense and offered me no benefit. In reality, the only documented evidence shows that he attempted to intimidate and coerce me into accepting it. Yet, the judge ignored this, and OLPR dismissed it as mere "sloppy representation."

Judge Diamond perpetuated this injustice by enforcing a settlement arrangement that was not supported by any evidence and defied reason. He imposed a higher standard of accountability on me than on Brian, Tim, or anyone else involved. When I directly questioned why Brian's lack of evidence was not a factor in his rulings, he chose to ignore me. Instead, he ruled as though Brian had presented legitimate proof. The ethical guidelines governing judicial conduct required him to report Brian to OLPR when he became aware of the police report against him. He failed to do so. Similarly, when Tim attempted to blackmail me, the judge should have reported it but didn't. His failure to uphold these ethical obligations undermined the fairness of my case.

He was still on probation when he filed his first motion against me, alleging that he was "irreparably harmed" because I had supposedly forced him to accept cash for his retainer. The evidence he submitted contradicted his own claims, yet neither the judge nor OLPR addressed the fact that he was blatantly lying to the court. His dishonesty should have been a clear probation violation, but instead, the legal system enabled him to continue.

No evidence. No factual basis for the court's rulings. No legitimate foundation for either of the so-called settlement agreements. No meaningful enforcement of the probation agreement. This entire process—draining resources, court costs, OLPR staff time, and attorney fees—amounted to an estimated $150,000 spent on a charade. And yet, no one has been willing to acknowledge the truth: that it was fundamentally wrong from the very beginning.

There is also another court transcript of a hearing of Brian sitting with his attorney talking about the number of times he was harmed – it was how he arrived at how he should be rewarded with $18,000. However, if you were to read the transcript, neither Brian nor his attorney actually stated anything specific about the harm – what it was that harmed him or why he was a victim.

I wanted Brian to be held accountable for his conduct, but his attorney actually filed a motion to the effect that holding him accountable for his conduct made him a victim. Somehow, this made sense to the judge and yet again, when I questioned it, I got ignored.

The systemic failures in my case were not isolated missteps but a clear pattern of negligence, dishonesty, and disregard for justice. At every level- the attorneys who took my money under the ruse of representing me, the oversight bodies meant to ensure ethical conduct, the judge responsible for fairness, and the very legal system designed to uphold truth—there was a blatant refusal to demand accountability. Evidence was ignored, lies were tolerated, and those entrusted with upholding justice instead enabled deceit. In any other profession, had someone done to me what Brian and Tim did, they would have lost their license. But Brian was on probation while he was filing false claims against me, and OLPR said it was okay. Tim lied to the court about a settlement arrangement that made no sense, and all I got was that it was "sloppy representation." The judge forced me into a settlement arrangement that's not even in the court transcript, and the judicial ethics committee supports him in doing that.

This wasn't just about the inappropriate conduct of more than one lawyer or a single unfair ruling; it was a demonstration of how easily the system protects its own at the expense of those it claims to serve. And the sad, sick, and twisted part of it all is that they are trying to convince me— and everyone else—that this is how the legal system is supposed to work. After all the time, money, and effort wasted on this farce, the most troubling reality remains: the truth was never given a chance to matter.

# Epilogue

I told Judge Diamond that if what I experienced in his courtroom was such a good thing, then others ought to know about it. It's not a secret that should be kept. He didn't object.

I told him that if I had to pay a judgment over a suit and a settlement arrangement that didn't make any sense and had no merit, this was how I was going to pay for it. Brian also got a copy of what I sent to the judge, so he was aware the book was coming out, too. I didn't hear anything from either of them about stopping the book.

To see more court documents and correspondence, vistit my website:

https://justiceunraveled.com

.